NCUA Board Message

On behalf of the National Credit Union Administration (NCUA), we are honored to present the NCUA Strategic Plan for the years 2014 – 2017.

Throughout the history of cooperative credit unions, ever-changing times presented great opportunities and challenges. The years 2014 – 2017 will be no exception. In the past, the credit union system consistently emerged from each challenge more capable and vibrant with increased capacity to serve its members.

The credit union system and NCUA face a new financial services environment with credit unions exerting an increasing influence on America's economy. This environment demands strong, effective, and balanced regulation to protect consumers without hampering credit union system growth and innovation.

NCUA's Strategic Plan 2014 – 2017 outlines how we will address a growing system where credit unions are offering new services, engaging in greater portfolio diversity, and presenting new risk challenges. These challenges include more and different products, diversified holdings, growing real estate concentration, rapid changes in technology, escalating threats to cyber-security and increasing member business loan portfolios. Each of these risks requires continual monitoring and mitigation strategies.

We will continue to focus on our workforce, processes, tools, and technology to accomplish our mission. NCUA's Strategic Plan 2014 – 2017 provides direction addressing the opportunities and challenges in each area. This includes replacing institutional knowledge lost with the retirement of long-tenured employees and providing contemporary training for all staff. Many staff has less than five years of experience with NCUA, so the training and quality control functions increase in importance.

The changing financial services environment is also driving a need for greater diversity of employee skills. This includes individuals with specialized expertise in capital markets, business lending, investments, information technology, cyber-security, economics, statistics and many other related fields. NCUA staff, our most important asset, must have the skills, training, and tools necessary to do their job in this more complex and dynamic financial environment.

Part of the strategic planning process includes assessing the tools and authorities at NCUA's disposal to fulfill its mission. While these are not included within the plan as a specific goal or objective, these legislative priorities are important to NCUA fulfilling its mission and supporting the goals and objectives in the plan. They include:

1. Providing NCUA with vendor authority through statutory changes that achieve parity with the other federal financial regulatory agencies to regulate, examine, and take enforcement actions against vendors and Credit Union Service Organizations (CUSOs).

2. Restoring NCUA's access to back-up liquidity. The specific statutory changes NCUA seeks include re-establishing NCUA's emergency borrowing authority of $30 billion which sunset on December 31, 2010, and revising Title III of the Federal Credit Union Act to modernize the Central Liquidity Facility.

3. Improving NCUA's ability to manage the NCUSIF by providing more flexibility in setting the normal operating level and building retained earnings for the NCUSIF in a manner consistent with the size, complexity and risk within the credit union industry.

NCUA and the credit union system are provided with many opportunities for success, but we also know each of these opportunities brings its own special challenges. This plan summarizes our analysis of the internal and external environment impacting credit unions and NCUA; evaluates our programs and risks; and provides the goals and objectives for the next four years.

Table of Contents

NCUA Board Message 2

Economic Outlook 5

Credit Union Industry Key Risks 7

Organizational Structure 8

Vision Statement 9

Mission Statement 9

Major Programs 9

Stakeholder Outreach 10

Management Priorities & Objectives 11

Agency Priority Goals 11

Cross-Agency Priority Goals 12

Strategic Goals & Objectives 13

    Strategic Goal 1 .... *15*

    Strategic Goal 2 .... *18*

    Strategic Goal 3 .... *21*

    Strategic Goal 4 .... *23*

Evaluations and Research 26

Economic Outlook

The economic environment exerts considerable influence on the credit union industry. As the economy continues to recover, lending opportunities should expand and credit risk should subside. An improving economy will likely be accompanied by rising interest rates, which will affect credit unions' income and balance sheets through a variety of channels. In the near term, key fiscal policy risks persist as policymakers continue developing a long-term solution.

Interest Rate Risk

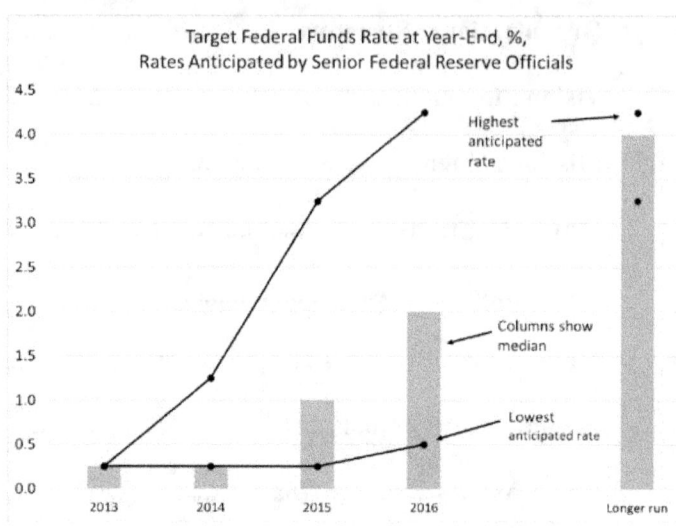

The current interest rate environment is unprecedented with short-term rates near zero for several years and long-term rates at historic lows. As a result, the size and speed of interest rate increases is uncertain, which is reflected in the wide range of opinions about the appropriate federal funds rate target (see chart) even among Federal Reserve policymakers. Interest rate increases have already begun; between April and August 2013, the monthly average of the 10-year Treasury increased nearly 100 basis points. The range of opinions also suggests interest rate volatility is likely to rise going forward. Credit unions should be prepared for interest rates to increase rapidly, but also for rates to swing sharply.

Guidance from the Federal Reserve indicates the pace of economic recovery will play a large role in determining when to begin to slow and then reverse a very accommodative policy. While the near-term policy timetable is uncertain, if the recovery continues, jobs increase, and the unemployment rate falls, the Federal Reserve will likely end its long-term asset purchases. During that time, longer-term interest rates will likely rise, though the path may not be smooth. If the economy continues to grow, short-term interest rates will likely be rising soon after Federal Reserve asset purchases end.

Forecasters project interest rates will rise over the next five years. The rate on the 10-year Treasury note, currently around 2.5 percent, is expected to be around 4.5 percent in 2017. Rising Treasury rates will lead to higher mortgage rates, curbing demand for mortgage loans.

While home purchase loans will likely continue to grow, rising rates will substantially reduce refinancing demand, which will directly reduce credit union income. According to 2012 data collected for the Home Mortgage Disclosure Act, 75 percent (by dollar volume) of credit union mortgage lending was refinancing loans. Credit unions relying on mortgage refinancing will need to find other income sources when interest rates rise and take advance action to mitigate interest rate risk.

Mortgages currently make up the majority of the credit union industry's loan portfolio, and long-term investments paying fixed interest rates have become a larger share of total assets. There is a risk that credit unions may find their loan and investment portfolios with a concentration in fixed rate securities with low rates not generating sufficient income to keep pace with expenses.

Interest rate risk will be a concern for even those credit unions that do not engage in mortgage lending or have a large component of fixed-rate assets. As short-term interest rates increase, credit unions with deposits concentrated in interest rate-sensitive accounts such as money market accounts will have to raise deposit rates or risk losing the deposits. Analysts have also suggested regular shares may be more sensitive to the expected increases as consumers seek to increase their income.

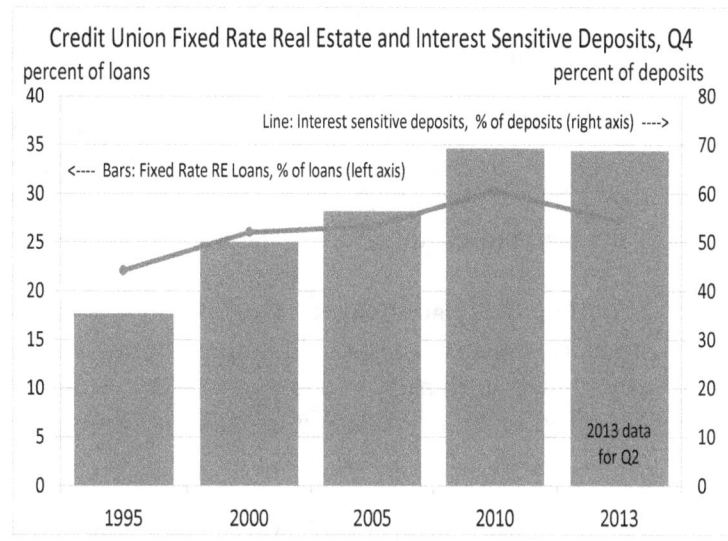

Federal Reserve policymakers generally project the economy will have recovered enough for the historically low short-term interest rates to rise in 2015. The net interest margin at credit unions has fallen in recent years and rising interest expenses could further exacerbate this trend, especially after 2014 when increases are expected to be concentrated in short-term rates. Lower net interest margins will put downward pressure on net worth leaving credit unions vulnerable to future economic shocks.

Key Risk Areas for U.S. Growth

While forecasters expect the American economy will grow over the medium term, there are several risks that could undermine this growth.

- Global Factors: Growth in the U.S. is partially dependent on growth in the rest of the world. Changes in crude oil supplies and prices also remain important. Recent information suggests growth around the world is improving. However, potential risk areas and uncertainty exist in Europe, Japan and the Middle East.

- Federal Budgets and Debt: While an improving economy and fiscal austerity helped reduce the federal budget deficit, the long-term imbalance between federal revenues and outlays can only be addressed through fundamental reforms. In the near term, key fiscal policy risks persist as policymakers continue to develop a long-term solution.

Credit Union Industry Key Risks

Evolving Interest Rate Environment: Interest rates are near historic lows and the transition to a more "normal" rate environment will pose challenges for some credit unions. Appropriate asset-liability management strategies are increasingly important as credit unions manage exposure to fixed-rate loans and long-term investments in a rapidly changing interest rate environment.

Cyber-Security: As online and mobile transactions become increasingly integrated into consumers' interaction with financial institutions, the risk of hacking and fraud will continue increasing. Credit unions will need to continually monitor and enhance the security of their systems to protect themselves and their members.

Third Party Relationships: More reliance is being placed on third parties to deliver products and services to credit union members. NCUA's lack of statutory authority over credit union third party vendors increases systemic risk from the relationships, particularly with Credit Union Service Organizations, which provide services to large concentrations of credit unions.

Lending and Investment Trends: High concentration in real estate and rapid growth in new areas like member business and student loans emphasize the need for effective risk management tools and practices.

Membership Trends: Demographic and field of membership composition changes are likely to mean credit unions will have to consider whether their product mix is consistent with the needs of current and future members. A balanced regulatory environment will be necessary to enable credit unions to provide an optimal mix of products in a safe and sound manner.

Labor Force Participation: Membership trends may be affected by declining labor force participation. Labor force participation has been declining due to both cyclical and structural changes. As "baby boomers" retire in greater numbers, deposit growth and loan demand may be limited over the next few years unless credit unions are successful in attracting younger members.

Consolidation Trends: Technological advances and demographic changes mean that more members will demand complex products and services that smaller credit unions will struggle to provide. These changes may increase the rate of industry consolidation going forward.

Alternative Loan and Depository Institutions: New financial products that mimic deposit accounts are appearing, including some from institutions that have little or no regulatory oversight. This is a challenge to consumer education. Credit unions may have to be more active in marketing and rethink their business models in response to this new source of competition.

Organizational Structure

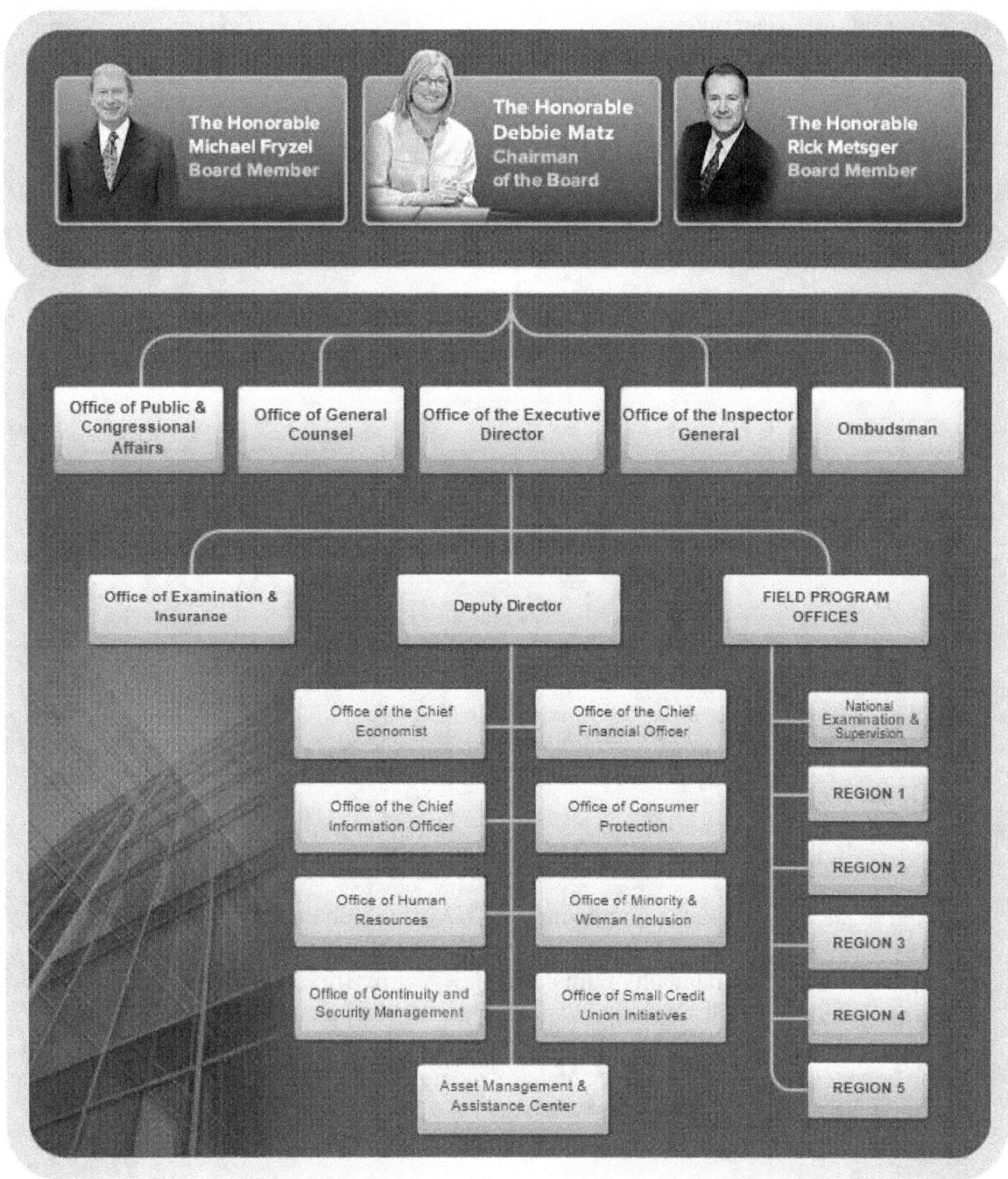

NCUA is the independent federal agency created by the U.S. Congress to regulate, charter, and supervise federal credit unions. With the backing of the full faith and credit of the U.S. Government, NCUA operates and manages the National Credit Union Share Insurance Fund (NCUSIF), insuring the deposits of the account holders in all federal credit unions and the overwhelming majority of state-chartered credit unions.

NCUA, through its predecessors, was created in 1934 with the passage of the Federal Credit Union Act. In 1934, the credit union system focused on enhancing the ability of its members to achieve their financial goals. Today, while many of the products and services are different, the credit union system maintains this same focus. The credit union system consistently assists their members through turmoil such as the Great Depression, World War II, the Great Recession of 2008, and natural disasters that occur each year.

As the products and services provided to members changed over the years, NCUA's supervision and regulation evolved as well. In 1970, this evolution included the addition of the NCUSIF providing the backing of the full faith and credit of the U.S. Government to credit union accounts bolstering the confidence of its members.

NCUA employs approximately 1,260 full time staff responsible for the regulation and supervision of 6,620 federally insured credit unions with nearly 96 million members across all states and U.S. territories.

Vision Statement

"NCUA will protect consumer rights and member deposits."

Mission Statement

"Provide, through regulation and supervision, a safe and sound credit union system, which promotes confidence in the national system of cooperative credit."

Major Programs

All program areas coordinate to implement NCUA's mission and vision. NCUA employs various operational processes to meet strategic goals including the periodic review of its operational structure to maintain optimal efficiency. All offices work to recruit highly qualified candidates to fill vacancies. Training and development provides staff with the knowledge, skills, and abilities to effectively implement NCUA's mission. NCUA uses leading edge technology to improve agency-wide communication and program efficiencies. The following are the major program areas.

Supervision
The supervision program contributes to the safety and soundness of the credit union system. A program priority includes identifying and resolving risk concerns such as interest rate risk, operational risks including cyber-security, credit risk, and reputational risk. NCUA supervises federally insured credit unions through examinations and regulatory enforcement including providing guidance through various publications and taking administrative actions as necessary to manage risk.

Insurance
NCUA manages the NCUSIF, which provides insurance for deposits held at federally insured credit unions. The fund is capitalized by credit unions. NCUA manages the fund to ensure member deposits are insured to at least $250,000.

Small Credit Union Initiatives
NCUA fosters credit union development, particularly the expansion of services provided by small credit unions to eligible members. This is addressed through consulting, training, partnerships and assistance. A major source of assistance is the Community Development Revolving Loan Fund (CDRLF), which provides loans and technical grants to credit unions serving low-income members to provide basic financial services and stimulate economic activities in their communities.

Consumer Protection
NCUA protects credit union members through effective enforcement of federal financial services consumer protection laws, regulations, and requirements. NCUA is developing and promoting financial literacy education programs for credit unions to assist members in making financial decisions.

Asset Management
NCUA conducts credit union liquidations and performs management and recovery of assets through its Asset Management and Assistance Center (AMAC). AMAC strives to maximize the recovery of assets in liquidations where fraud occurred. AMAC assists NCUA regional offices with the review of large, complex loan portfolios and actual or potential bond claims. It also participates extensively in the operational phases of conservatorships and records reconstruction. The purpose of AMAC is to minimize costs to the NCUSIF and credit union members.

Stakeholder Outreach

In order to clearly understand the needs of the credit union system, NCUA seeks input from all of its stakeholders, including Congress, credit union members, credit unions and their associations. Input is sought through our examination and supervision process, surveys, public webinars, working groups, rulemakings, and public and congressional dialogue. The views and input are assessed and properly considered during the developmental process. For this plan, this input may influence directly or indirectly the goals or objectives, the selection of measures of success, and the performance targets.

Management Priorities & Objectives

To fully implement NCUA's mission, the following are NCUA priorities that factor into the strategic plan. These priorities were established by Chairman Matz in 2009 and have been the core theme of NCUA's actions since that time. These priorities will enable NCUA to continue to address industry changes and they provide the core of the four goals in this plan. The priorities include:

1. Recognized as a fair, effective regulator that sets the highest standards for safety and soundness (Goal 1).

2. An advocate of initiatives to protect members from predatory, unsafe financial products (Goal 2).

3. A regulator that ensures access to credit union service for all eligible members (Goal 2).

4. An agency that listens and encourages an exchange of ideas with the credit union industry while maintaining its independence (Goal 3).

5. A model corporate citizen that recognizes its responsibility to implement environmentally sound practices and procedures wherever and whenever feasible (Goal 3 & 4).

6. An employer of choice and will foster positive relations with elected labor representatives (Goal 4).

Agency Priority Goals

OMB encourages all agencies to prioritize goals in their strategic and annual plans. An Agency Priority Goal (APG) is a subset of the agency's performance goals and represents the highest implementation priorities. An APG is a near-term result or achievement to accomplish within approximately 24 months. NCUA identifies six performance goals as APGs in this Strategic Plan. NCUA's Annual Performance Plan provides more detail on each of the APGs.

1. Implement a robust supervision framework for NCUA's financial-reform regulations including interest rate risk, liquidity and contingency funding plans, derivative authority, and capital planning and stress testing, as outlined under Strategic Objective 1.2.

2. Issue industry guidance related to emerging cyber-security risks and related threats, as outlined under Strategic Objective 1.4.

3. Monitor issues or trends in consumer complaints to develop effective financial literacy education programs and initiatives, as outlined under Strategic Objective 2.3.

4. Develop guidance to the credit union system to provide explanation of regulatory changes and best practices for implementation, as outlined under Strategic Objective 3.4.

5. Increase the number of women and minority staff at all levels particularly in the management ranks, as outlined under Strategic Objective 4.3.

6. Strengthen the security program in the areas of personnel, facilities, continuity of operation and secure communications, as outlined under Strategic Objective 4.6.

Cross-Agency Priority Goals

The Government Performance and Results Modernization Act requires federal agencies to address Cross-Agency Priority (CAP) Goals in their strategic plan, annual performance plan, and annual performance report. The national level CAP Goals are located at www.Performance.gov. While NCUA is an independent federal agency and not part of the federal budget, it contributes toward four CAP Goals; Cyber-Security, Closing Skills Gap (among federal work force), Sustainability (greeNCUA), and Open Government Data.

NCUA is involved in numerous cross agency initiatives by collaborating with the other federal financial regulatory agencies through participation in several councils. Significant councils include the Financial Stability Oversight Council (FSOC), the Federal Financial Institutions Examination Council (FFIEC), and the OMB Performance Improvement Council. While NCUA does not have specific cross agency priority goals, these councils and many associated task forces and working groups contribute to the success of NCUA's mission.

Strategic Goals & Objectives

The chart below summarizes NCUA's strategic goals and objectives. Strategic objectives reflect the outcome or impact of the broader strategic goals. Senior executives are appointed as the goal leader for each strategic goal. They are responsible for managing the strategic goal and corresponding objectives.

Strategic Goals	*Strategic Objectives*
Goal 1: Ensure a Safe, Sound, and Sustainable Credit Union System	1.1 Identify, measure, monitor, and mitigate levels of risk in the credit union industry through effective regulations, supervision, and examination. 1.2 Manage operational vulnerabilities resulting from new products and services, especially shifts in balance sheet composition. 1.3 Implement tools and models for evaluation and assessment of industry-wide risks. 1.4 Be prepared for and promote awareness of critical risk issues, emerging technologies, and related threats. 1.5 Increase ability to manage risk through an effective examination and supervision program that minimizes loss to the NCUSIF.
Goal 2: Promote Consumer Protection and Financial Literacy	2.1 Establish a framework of well-balanced regulations and policy statements. 2.2 Ensure federally insured credit unions comply with rules and regulations established to protect consumers. 2.3 Develop and promote financial literacy education programs to empower consumers to make informed financial decisions. 2.4 Promote access to federally insured financial services for consumers of all backgrounds and income levels. 2.5 Review marketing and business plans of community charters to ensure progress toward meeting stated goals. 2.6 Educate credit unions about consumer compliance issues.
Goal 3: Further Develop a Regulatory Environment that is Transparent and Effective, with Clearly Articulated and Easily Understood Regulations	3.1 Reduce unnecessary obstacles to credit union competitiveness through modernized regulations. 3.2 Collaborate with other regulators to discuss strategies and goals for implementing new or revised regulations. 3.3 Maintain a regulatory environment that safeguards member interests and stability in the credit union system. 3.4 Enhance NCUA's communication with credit unions through transparent regulations and guidance.

Goal 4: Cultivate an Environment that Fosters a Diverse, Well-Trained and Motivated Staff	*4.1 Develop and maintain the optimal knowledge, skills, and abilities of the agency's workforce to meet emerging needs.* 4.2 Enhance staff effectiveness and efficiency through the use of technology. 4.3 Recruit and retain a well-diversified and highly qualified workforce that reflects the relevant labor force. 4.4 Maintain an effective plan of succession to ensure continuity of leadership throughout all levels of the organization. 4.5 Improve NCUA's internal communication, both horizontally and vertically. 4.6 Enhance NCUA's position as one of the best places in the government to work.

Strategic Goal 1

Ensure a Safe, Sound, and Sustainable Credit Union System

Goal Leader	Strategic Goal Overview
Director of the Office of Examination and Insurance	NCUA's primary function is to identify credit union industry risks, determine the magnitude, and mitigate unacceptable levels through the examination and supervision program. Industry risks include interest rate risk, operational risks including cyber-security, credit risk, and reputation risk. NCUA addresses emerging issues in order to minimize losses to the NCUSIF.

Performance Goals

The performance goals below will be pursued as a means to achieve our strategic goals and objectives. The annual performance goals, measures, and targets are provided in NCUA's 2014 Annual Performance Plan.

Strategic Objective 1.1 - Identify, measure, monitor, and mitigate levels of risk in the credit union industry through effective regulations, supervision, and examination.

- Maintain strong levels of credit union system-wide net worth and corporate credit union leverage ratios.

- Improve the number of rehabilitated problem credit unions (CAMEL Composite Codes 3, 4, and 5) as a percentage of problem credit unions.

- Examine all federal credit unions annually.

- Examine all federally insured state credit unions with assets above $250 million annually.

Strategic Objective 1.2 - Manage operational vulnerabilities resulting from new products and services, especially shifts in balance sheet composition.

- Implement a robust supervision framework for NCUA's financial reform regulations including interest rate risk, liquidity and contingency funding plans, derivatives authority, and capital planning and stress testing *(Agency Priority Goal)*.

- Update the automated examination system to incorporate economic model analysis.

Strategic Objective 1.3 - Implement tools and models for evaluation and assessment of industry-wide risks.

- Employ business intelligence tools to identify and monitor risks to the credit union industry.

Strategic Objective 1.4 - Be prepared for and promote awareness of critical risk issues, emerging technologies, and related threats.

- Identify regional and national emerging risks requiring necessary actions.

- Issue industry guidance related to emerging cyber-security risks and related threats *(Agency*

Priority Goal).

- Provide training in emerging technologies, especially for field and management staff.
- Assist small and low-income credit unions to secure the proper technology and resources to ensure regulatory compliance and avoid any potential negative threats.

Strategic Objective 1.5 - **Increase ability to manage risk through an effective examination and supervision program that minimizes loss to the NCUSIF.**

- Maintain yearly NCUSIF losses as a percentage of total insured shares.
- Minimize total assets in CAMEL Code 4/5 rated credit unions.

Context
Strategic Goal 1 objectives focus on minimizing current and future risks as early as possible and encouraging sustainability within the system.

Strategies
<ul><li>Increase the ability to identify, measure, and monitor risk more effectively through the supervision program by improving risk analysis and continuing to develop risk management tools.</li><li>Identify, measure, and monitor operational and technological related vulnerabilities resulting from new products and services at both macro and micro levels through on-site and off-site monitoring tools.</li><li>Promote awareness of critical risk issues through issued guidance and training.</li><li>Ensure timely resolution of problem institutions through the examination and supervision process to minimize losses to the NCUSIF.</li></ul>

Contributing Offices
<ul><li>Office of National Examination and Supervision</li><li>All Regional Offices</li><li>Office of Small Credit Union Initiatives</li><li>Office of Consumer Protection</li><li>Office of Chief Economist</li><li>Office of Chief Information Officer</li><li>Asset Management and Assistance Center</li></ul>

External Factors
External factors which may affect Goal 1 achievement include:<ul><li>Complexity of and consumer demand for new credit union products and services.</li><li>Regulatory requirements with unintended burdens.</li><li>Reputation risk amongst NCUA stakeholders and the public.</li></ul>

- Economic conditions.
- Accounting changes that may negatively affect the credit union system's net worth.
- Competitive pressures from other financial service providers.
- Velocity of risk taking by credit unions impacting balance sheet structure, credit risk, and concentration risk.

Strategic Goal 2

Promote Consumer Protection and Financial Literacy

Goal Leader	Strategic Goal Overview
Director of the Office of Consumer Protection	Strategic Goal 2 seeks to ensure a regulatory framework exists to provide consumers appropriate and timely disclosures, sufficient protections against unscrupulous products or services, and financial literacy education programs to help consumers make informed financial decisions.

Performance Goals

The performance goals below will be pursued as a means to achieve our strategic goals and objectives. The annual performance goals, measures, and targets are provided in NCUA's 2014 Annual Performance Plan.

Strategic Objective 2.1 - **Establish a framework of well-balanced regulations and policy statements.**

- Collaborate and consult with other federal regulators on consumer financial protection issues and potential regulations.
- Solicit information on potential abusive or deceptive practices through various outreach efforts.

Strategic Objective 2.2 - **Ensure federally insured credit unions comply with rules and regulations established to protect consumers.**

- Complete the risk-based fair lending exam procedures and exam scoping steps to measure credit union compliance with consumer financial protection regulations.
- Ensure quality control reviews of fair lending examination reports highlight potential consumer compliance issues and follow-up for needed corrective actions.
- Increase guidance to the credit union industry to help reduce the number of compliance violations.

Strategic Objective 2.3 - **Develop and promote financial literacy education programs to empower consumers to make informed financial decisions.**

- Monitor issues or trends in consumer complaints to develop effective financial literacy education programs and initiatives *(Agency Priority Goal)*.
- Partner with outside resources to effectively market the availability of financial literacy programs.

Strategic Objective 2.4 - **Promote access to federally insured financial services for consumers of all backgrounds and income levels.**

- Notify credit unions of their eligibility for low-income status.
- Continue to increase usability and contemporary information on MyCreditUnion.gov, including Pocket Cents.

- Increase availability of non-English materials on NCUA websites.

Strategic Objective 2.5 - Review marketing and business plans of community charters to ensure progress toward meeting stated goals.

- Ensure community charter penetration rate, loans, shares, and other member services are consistent with credit union submitted community charter business plans.

Strategic Objective 2.6 - Educate credit unions about consumer compliance issues.

- Use all available delivery channels to provide information on consumer compliance related guidance and information.

Context
Strategic Goal 2 objectives provide the actions to help protect consumer rights and member deposits by establishing appropriate regulations, enhancing consumer confidence, and providing financial literacy and education.

Strategies
<ul><li>Collaborate with the other federal regulatory agencies as appropriate, to maintain a safe and sound regulatory environment to protect consumers using credit union products and services.</li><li>Support credit unions in their efforts to offer essential products and services, including financial education programs to all eligible members, especially those of modest means.</li><li>Structure the Community Development Revolving Loan Fund Program (CDRLF) to emphasize credit unions' outreach and financial services to low-income communities.</li><li>Uphold public confidence in the NCUSIF.</li><li>Review credit union compliance with their community charter business plan.</li><li>Use all available media outlets to promote consumer rights.</li></ul>

Contributing Offices
<ul><li>Office of Examination and Insurance</li><li>Office of National Examination and Supervision</li><li>Office of Small Credit Union Initiatives</li><li>Office of Public and Congressional Affairs</li><li>All Regional Offices</li></ul>

External Factors
External factors which may affect Goal 2 achievement include:<ul><li>Changes in credit union membership growth rates, member needs, or fields of membership.</li><li>Lack of public awareness about the benefits of credit union membership.</li><li>A shift in member needs due to changing demographics of membership.</li></ul>

- A declining number of credit unions.
- Competitive pressures from other financial service providers.
- Legislative changes.

Strategic Goal 3

Further Develop a Regulatory Environment that is Transparent and Effective, with Clearly Articulated and Easily Understood Regulations

Goal Leader	Strategic Goal Overview
General Counsel	NCUA strives to effectively manage the balance between regulatory flexibility and responsible oversight. NCUA's goal is to issue simple, clear, and straightforward regulations while addressing emerging issues before they become major problems.

Performance Goals

The performance goals below will be pursued as a means to achieve our strategic goals and objectives. The annual performance goals, measures, and targets are provided in NCUA's 2014 Annual Performance Plan.

Strategic Objective 3.1 - **Reduce unnecessary obstacles to credit union competitiveness through modernized regulations.**

- Update existing and develop new regulations through the annual regulatory review process.
- Coordinate with congressional committees on priority risk issues.
- Identify industry risks necessitating new or revised regulations in industry guidance.

Strategic Objective 3.2 - **Collaborate with other regulators to discuss strategies and goals for implementing new or revised regulations.**

- Actively participate in financial regulators meetings to contribute to the development and implementation of industry guidance.

Strategic Objective 3.3 - **Maintain a regulatory environment that safeguards member interests and stability in the credit union system.**

- Provide sufficient comment periods when introducing new or revised regulations and consider public comments when finalizing regulations.

Strategic Objective 3.4 - **Enhance NCUA's communication with credit unions through transparent regulations and guidance.**

- Develop guidance to credit unions to provide explanation of regulatory changes and best practices for implementation *(Agency Priority Goal)*.
- Increase target audience awareness of regulatory activities and their positive effects on the industry's safety and soundness.
- Issue information on new and changed regulations through multiple delivery channels including the NCUA website, Twitter, Facebook, LinkedIn, and YouTube.

Context

These objectives support NCUA's focus on being an effective financial regulator which includes keeping pace with innovation that manifests through new products, services, and technology while minimizing risk to the NCUSIF.

Strategies

- Communicate with stakeholders to address potential regulatory obstacles and allow for credit union competitiveness.
- Actively collaborate with other regulators to successfully develop and implement new or revised regulations.
- Develop regulations to address emerging risks while protecting member interests and minimizing NCUSIF losses.
- Communicate new and revised regulations including supervisory intent to stakeholders to ensure transparency.

Contributing Offices

- Office of Examination and Insurance
- Office of Consumer Protection
- Office of National Examination and Supervision
- Office of Minority and Woman Inclusion
- Office of Small Credit Union Initiatives
- Office of Public and Congressional Affairs

External Factors

External factors which may affect Goal 3 achievement include:

- Legislative changes and regulations expanding supervisory responsibilities and impacting the credit union system.
- Complexity of financial services facilitated by technology and member demands.
- Innovation resulting in new products and services.

Strategic Goal 4

Cultivate an Environment that Fosters a Diverse, Well-Trained and Motivated Staff

Goal Leader	Strategic Goal Overview
Deputy Executive Director	NCUA's most important resource is high quality, skilled staff. To maximize their contributions to the mission, they must be supported by efficient and effective processes and have the tools and leading edge technology.

Performance Goals

The performance goals below will be pursued as a means to achieve our strategic goals and objectives. The annual performance goals, measures, and targets are provided in NCUA's 2014 Annual Performance Plan.

Strategic Objective 4.1 - **Develop and maintain the optimal knowledge, skills, and abilities of the agency's workforce to meet emerging needs.**

- Use all available delivery channels to educate staff on new and updated guidance and regulations.
- Deliver quality training consistent with the various staff areas of discipline.

Strategic Objective 4.2 - **Enhance staff effectiveness and efficiency through the use of technology.**

- Develop specialized systems, tools, and models to create a more effective examination program.
- Deliver leading edge information technology hardware and software to maximize staff efficiency.
- Increase virtual, remote and telework employee efficiency through the use of current technology.

Strategic Objective 4.3 - **Recruit and retain a well-diversified and highly qualified workforce that reflects the relevant labor force.**

- Increase the number of women, persons with disabilities, and minority staff at all levels particularly in the management ranks *(Agency Priority Goal)*.
- Partner with organizations to increase the diversity of NCUA staff, particularly management.
- Fill vacancies timely with the best-qualified applicants available.

Strategic Objective 4.4 - **Maintain an effective plan of succession to ensure continuity of leadership throughout all levels of the organization.**

- Capture valuable institutional knowledge of retiring senior executives.
- Enhance leadership training programs to provide continued education for all levels of staff.

Strategic Objective 4.5 - Improve NCUA's internal communication, both horizontally and vertically.

- Provide clear and timely communication between all levels of staff.
- Coordinate agency communications to maintain consistent strategic messaging.

Strategic Objective 4.6 - Enhance NCUA's position as one of the best places in the government to work.

- Solicit staff input on areas requiring attention.
- Strive to balance organizational needs with comparability with the other financial regulatory agencies in the areas of pay and benefits.
- Streamline operation policies and practices to reduce administrative burden for all staff.
- Strengthen the security program in the areas of personnel, facilities, continuity of operation and secure communications *(Agency Priority Goal)*.

Context

Strategic Goal 4 emphasizes staff effectiveness through hiring, training, and career development. It also focuses on maintaining sufficient levels of communication and preparing staff to assume additional responsibilities and duties in leadership positions. The goal also covers the need for high quality administrative and support functions for all staff.

Strategies

- Develop and maintain the knowledge, skills, and abilities of the agency's workforce to consistently identify and meet emerging needs.
- Recruit and retain a highly qualified workforce that reflects the labor force.
- Maintain strong executive and management development programs to ensure the continuity of leadership and agency efficiency and effectiveness.
- Maintain high quality performance in all administrative and support functions impacting staff and external stakeholders.

Contributing Offices

- Office of Human Resources
- Office of the Chief Information Officer
- Office of the Chief Financial Officer
- Office of Minority and Women Inclusion
- Office of Continuity and Security Management
- Note that all offices contribute to the hiring and training of staff and succession planning

External Factors
External factors which may affect Goal 4 achievement include: • Access to a qualified labor pool and maintenance of a skilled workforce (such as increased competition for talent). • Ability to retain talent (including quality of life, travel burdens, and upward mobility). • Pace of change in financial marketplace may increase the need to rapidly adapt training and skills to meet emerging needs. • Impending retirement wave and loss of institutional knowledge.

Evaluations and Research

NCUA uses program evaluations as an integral part of its effort to continuously improve and enhance mission performance. Both external and internal entities evaluate NCUA's performance using a variety of tools. The principal external and internal evaluations are listed below.

General Accountability Office (GAO) evaluations are performed as necessary. The GAO conducts program and program support related evaluations of NCUA.

Financial audits are conducted annually by an outside audit firm contracted by the **Office of the Inspector General (OIG)**. The firm audits the NCUA Operations Fund, National Credit Union Share Insurance Fund, Temporary Corporate Credit Union Stabilization Fund, Central Liquidity Facility, and the Community Development Revolving Loan Fund.

The **Federal Information Security Management Act (FISMA)** evaluation is the annual review and evaluation of NCUA's information technology systems. This includes evaluating IT controls for financial management systems.

OIG evaluations and **Material Loss Reviews** are conducted throughout the year. These independent evaluations are performed in accordance with OIG procedures and include reviews of NCUA programs and program support operations.

A federal **Employee Viewpoint Survey** is conducted annually by the Office of Personnel Management (OPM). The survey measures the opinions of NCUA staff on a wide range of topics.

www.ingramcontent.com/pod-product-compliance
Lightning Source LLC
Chambersburg PA
CBHW081824170526
45167CB00008B/3531